Moving Forward on Your Own

This book is provided as a gift to you from

_____

along with

Protect Tomorrow. Embrace Today.™

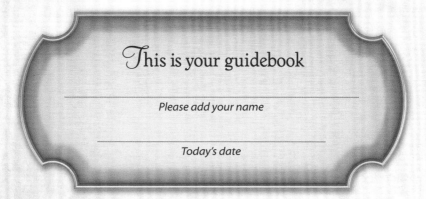

This is your guidebook

_____
Please add your name

_____
Today's date

"In everyone's life, at some time, our inner fire
goes out…and is rekindled by a spark from
another person. Each of us has cause to think
with deep gratitude of those who have
lighted the flame within us."

~*Albert Schweitzer*

Moving Forward on Your Own

REVISED EDITION

A Financial Guidebook *for* Widows

KATHLEEN M. REHL, Ph.D., CFP®

REHL FINANCIAL ADVISORS | LAND O'LAKES, FLORIDA

Published by:

REHL FINANCIAL ADVISORS

Land O'Lakes, Florida 34639

To order additional copies of this guidebook, please visit www.kathleenrehl.com.

Text ©2010 Kathleen M. Rehl, Ph.D., CFP®

Paintings ©2010 Patrick J. Gaughan, artist

Photos ©2010 Stanley L. Moore, Stan Moore Photography

Cover and interior design by Monica Thomas
for TLC Graphics, www.TLCGraphics.com

Library of Congress Control Number: 2010906189
ISBN-13: 978-0-9845793-0-3

Printed in the United States of America
REVISED EDITION PRINTING: 2013

This guidebook has received several book awards

Dedication

Many people have influenced my journey, including friends, clients, teachers, authors, and family members. This guidebook is dedicated to two special widows I loved greatly during their lifetimes — my mother, Mary Elizabeth, and my grandmother, Ruth. They were great role models when it was my turn to become a widow.

I also dedicate this book to Tom, my dear late husband, who taught me so much. He was my best friend and soulmate. I've felt his encouraging spirit with me throughout the creation of this guidebook. Tom's positive presence will continue to inspire me to pursue my dreams and live a meaningful life, despite the heartache accompanying his passing.

I thank all three of you for the beautiful and unconditional love you gave me during your lifetimes. You were the best!

"People gain so much hope when
they know they are not experiencing
something alone."

~*Joyce Rupp*

Table of Contents

"Far away there in the sunshine are my highest
aspirations. I may not reach them, but I can look
up and see their beauty, believe in them, and try to
follow where they lead."

~Louisa May Alcott

Acknowledgments

Thanks to the wonderful support from colleagues, clients, family, and friends who encouraged me to complete this guidebook. I especially appreciate the photography by Stanley L. Moore, my beloved brother. And special thanks to my friend and artist, Patrick J. Gaughan. I appreciate my wonderful staff, Kathy Alvare and Melody Ossi, who helped to make this project possible. My editor, Anne Lesser, provided great suggestions. I'm deeply grateful for the assistance of Tamara Dever and her TLC Graphics and Narrow Gate Books staff, who facilitated the guidebook's design and printing. A big thanks also to my colleagues at the Alliance of Cambridge Advisors, including Chip Simon, Karen Folk, and Judy Stewart, who helped me shape ideas for this guidebook. I will always be especially grateful to Bert Whitehead, from whom I've learned so much about how to make a difference in the lives of my clients.

Introduction

Right now you may be wondering, "Can I make it on my own without my husband?" You are not alone in your feelings, which some widows describe as "being in a fog." If you feel adrift and insecure in many ways, including financially, you are quite normal.

You might have found this guidebook by yourself. Or perhaps you are in a widow's support group using it together. Maybe a professional recommended the guidebook and will work with you on certain sections. Or did a friend give it to you as a gift? Possibly you received this guidebook from a hospice counselor or a funeral home director. In whatever way you acquired your book, you will find it is a useful tool to help with your financial transitions.

I hope this book will serve as a catalyst to help you move forward after your spouse's death. Every year, hundreds of thousands of women lose their partners. For example, there are a million baby boomer widows in the United States, and this number continues to rise significantly each year.

"Fulfilled life is possible in spite of unfulfilled wishes."

~Dietrich Bonhoeffer

I believe that by using this guidebook, you will begin to feel more secure about your financial matters.

The purpose of this book is not to teach you everything about money and financial planning. Rather, the guidebook invites you to look at your money issues in a way that builds confidence, so you won't be fearful about your financial future.

This guidebook is unique in several ways. It integrates basic financial information with self-reflective exercises about your finances, in an encouraging way that's not overwhelming. Beautiful artwork and inspirational quotes may also help heal your soul as you focus on your money issues.

Many pages encourage you to write a personal reflection as you think about the topics discussed. You are invited to take small positive steps forward. It's a way to start feeling more assured about your money issues without being burdened with a lot of difficult technical information.

Skim through the entire guidebook for a quick overall feel for its layout. Enjoy the paintings and photos before looking closely at the text. Read some of the inspirational quotations interspersed along the way. If you are a recent widow, you may want to start with the section "What to Do When Your Husband Dies." There are helpful checklists for initial steps to take as your life begins to stabilize.

Find a comfortable place to sit and read "Kathleen's Story." Then write your own story in the space provided. Maybe you'll relate a special memory during your married life. Perhaps you will describe how you are doing right now. You might even write a love note to your spouse, telling him you are trying to move ahead with your life. It's OK to keep a tissue box close by as you write.

Read this guidebook at your own pace — a page or so at a time — rather than finishing it all quickly. If you are reading the book along with the guidance of a professional or in a group class, you may be directed to certain sections. You don't have to read the pages sequentially, so you can move through the contents as you like.

Be gentle with yourself as you make progress with your emotional and financial well-being. I wish you the best on your new financial journey!

Blessings,

Kathleen

CONNECTING BRIDGE
STANLEY L. MOORE

Emotions
and Grief

"Gratitude for the present moment
and the fullness of life now is the
true prosperity."

~Eckhart Tolle

He's Gone ... Forever

It wasn't supposed to turn out this way. When you married, you both promised it would last "forever."

But it didn't. And now you are part of a growing demographic. Like your many other widowed "sisters," years ago you didn't think much about the fact that you would probably outlive your husband — most wives do. Or perhaps he succumbed to a terrible disease or accident at an early age. Maybe he died in service to our country while in the military.

This guidebook will help you move forward with money issues you're facing now. It's designed as a practical tool. These ideas have helped other women who also had to deal with money matters on their own.

You are not alone.

Kathleen's Story

My best friend, lover, co-parent, business partner, and husband died of liver cancer on February 12, 2007 — 11 weeks after his diagnosis and shortly before our 19th wedding anniversary. Tom died in my arms, at sunset in our home. Back then, I felt it was the end of my life, too.

Half of me was ripped off and thrown away at Tom's death. I felt that I had lost my identity with my partner's departure. Life would never be the same again. Yes, friends and family were there to support me, but my life partner was gone forever. I wanted to crawl into the casket with Tom at the funeral.

In my less than stellar state, I had to start taking care of all the necessary stuff after my husband's death. Sure, as a professional financial advisor I had helped other new widows with these same tasks, but that was different. It was me now. The work seemed overwhelming. I hated doing all these necessary things at the same time I was starting to accept the fact that my love was never going to walk through our front door again.

During the first weeks after Tom's death, I functioned in a daze. I cried a lot. Sleep was fitful at best. I couldn't figure out which side of the bed to sleep on without his strong arms around me. I would wake up in the middle of so many nights, certain his death was just a dream. But then the truth always came crashing in on me again. I couldn't eat. I couldn't concentrate and was forgetful. Where did I put my keys?

Suddenly I had new roles to perform that had always been Tom's responsibilities. I was clueless about how to get our car serviced, use the gas grill, adjust the lawn watering equipment, and so much more. I was mad at myself for not learning how to do these things while my husband was still alive.

As silly as it may sound, even though I'm a *Certified Financial Planner*™ professional, I experienced a few temporary fears about money. Without his Social Security check and his other consulting income, I also knew I would face greater expenses in the future when I looked at my reduced income and the bills piling up. Plus, I had lost my business partner. But when I started taking control of my financial future, I felt better. It helped a lot to develop a new financial road map designed around my much-changed situation.

I'm now in my fourth year of widowhood. Tom's death certainly was not an experience I expected to happen shortly after my 60th birthday, but I have grown and continue to learn on my journey of widowhood. I can't go back to my former life and the man I loved.

"I will keep moving forward,
and I'm here to encourage you to
do the same as you make progress
in your new life ahead."
~Kathleen M. Rehl

Cascading Emotions

When a woman's husband dies, she can experience a range of emotions. You may have felt some of these same feelings when your spouse passed on.

Those feelings don't go away instantly. Indeed, when you start working with money issues after your life partner is gone, you may feel emotionally overwhelmed.

What you are feeling is normal. You are not going crazy!

Have you experienced any of these feelings or others?

Numb • Lost

Emotionally Drained

Abandoned • Paralyzed • Lonely

Fragile • Angry • Weak • Aimless

Forgetful Helpless • Frightened

Overwhelmed • Disconnected

Vulnerable • Relieved

Pained • Guilty

Disoriented

"My husband's death was the most traumatic event in my life."

~ *Claire, a recent widow*

"What lies behind us and what lies in
front of us are but tiny matters as
compared to what lies within us."

~Ralph Waldo Emerson

Your Story

*Here's a place for you to describe what you've been through and
how you are feeling after the death of your husband.*

Grief and Mourning

Most widows experience various phases of grief and mourning, which are not necessarily sequential. You may go forward several steps and then slip back again. Reading this list, do any of these stages feel familiar to you?

Shock/numbness — You are shocked with your situation, even if your husband's death was anticipated following a long illness.

Confusion — You feel disoriented even in familiar surroundings. You may forget names of acquaintances or the location of items.

Denial — You could wake from a dream, imagining your husband is just in the next room. Or you wait for him to come through the front door at the end of the day.

Bargaining — You promise that if your spouse could still be alive, you would be a better wife, give him more attention, do more activities together, etc.

Anxiety — You worry about what lies ahead. You may also experience physical ramifications of anxiety, including back pain, headaches, difficulty in breathing, or weight change.

Anger — You feel angry with yourself or your friends who still have their partners. You may also be mad at your husband for leaving you behind or for not teaching you how to use the gas barbecue grill while he was alive.

Guilt — You wish you had spent more time with your husband having fun and enjoying each other. You may also feel guilty about events surrounding his death.

Depression — Your sadness comes and goes. You'll probably always feel some level of sorrow for his death long after he's gone.

Lonely and vulnerable — The house without his presence, the dinner table without his placemat, family and social gatherings without his laughter leave you feeling so alone. At this same time, you can also suspect that others may try to take advantage of you as a widow. (Listen to your intuition because there are those who prey on widows.)

False sense of overconfidence — After some time you may think you're a strong woman and are completely ready to move on. Be careful about taking risky actions at this critical juncture before you truly have a firm foundation. That's because you may fall backward temporarily and wonder if you can ever make real progress.

Acceptance — You're ready to move on, having accepted your situation. Some widows take a long time to reach this stage; others get there earlier.

Save major money decisions until a time when grief and mourning don't feel so overwhelming. It may also help to ask a trusted friend or relative to help with some decisions until you feel more stable.

◆ Which of these stages have you experienced? _____

_____

_____

_____

_____

_____

_____

_____

_____

◆ Who can you ask to give a second opinion on your money plans?

_____

_____

FEMININE TRIO

PATRICK J. GAUGHAN

Financial Steps for Recent Widows

"The future belongs to those
who believe in their dreams."

~Eleanor Roosevelt

What to Do When Your Husband Dies
Financial Steps for Recent Widows

When your husband dies, you may be faced with a terrible shadow of grief, fear, and uncertainty.

Just when you feel least able to cope with life, when you are low on mental and physical energy, you have many decisions to make that can permanently affect you: your finances, your family, your livelihood, and so much more.

It might seem no one really understands what you are going through. But there are immediate concerns to take care of after your spouse's death, including the funeral or memorial service. Then you'll deal with critical issues, including settling his estate and collecting death benefits. You used to make choices with your partner, but now you feel alone.

Review these items with members of your support network in the days, weeks, and months during the first year after your husband's passing. Only time will help to heal the grief you experience. Organizing your finances and taking the right steps will help you regain a sense of control, well-being, and reduced financial worry during your time of healing.

My blessings are with you as you begin to move forward in your journey, following a new path.

"Be content to progress in slow steps until you have legs to run and wings with which to fly."

~Padre Pio

Funeral/memorial period:

❑ Follow directives if body or organ donation was planned.

❑ Select a funeral home, if not already arranged.

❑ Discuss costs with the funeral director with the assistance of a family member or friend. Select what is within your budget. Order preprinted thank-you cards.

❑ Decide on cremation or burial, if not already determined.

❑ Make arrangements for the service, in consultation with your minister, priest, or rabbi if appropriate.

❑ Write an obituary and send it to local newspapers. Include information about memorial gifts if you prefer. A family member or friend can help you follow guidelines supplied by your local newspapers. The funeral home will also assist if requested.

❑ Notify friends, relatives, and others.

❑ Order at least 15 copies of the death certificate from the funeral director or health department.

❑ Allow family and close friends to assist with food preparation and housekeeping tasks.

❑ Arrange care for young children, if needed.

❑ Make a list of contacts you can reach in an emergency.

❑ Set up a system to record and later acknowledge cards, letters, phone calls, food, and other gifts.

Begin to organize information:

❑ Start a filing system for quick and easy retrieval of information you'll reference during this transition period. For example, use colored manila folders. Here are some possible file headings: bank correspondence, bills, credit card statements, business related, employer correspondence, estate documents, household, income tax related, investments, life insurance, other assets, and personal documents.

❑ Create a calendar with important due dates.

❑ Keep a log of actions taken, including the date and contact person if someone else was involved and pertinent notes. (If you don't create a list, you're likely to forget the dozens of contacts you'll make and things you have done.)

Contact your attorney, tax preparer and financial advisor:

❑ Gather significant documents, including your husband's will and trust if applicable.

❑ If you have not previously worked with a tax preparation professional, inquire about which documents to keep and your pertinent tax issues for the current year.

❑ Ask friends or a professional advisor for names of lawyers who do estate work if you don't already have an attorney. This person will guide you during the probate process.

❑ If you're the executor of your husband's will, manage the estate settlement process with the guidance of your professional advisors. Also see page 27 for estate settlement information.

❑ Share concerns about money issues with your financial advisor. If you don't have a financial planner and would like to talk about your circumstances, see page 74, "Finding a Financial Advisor."

Review cash flow and liquidity needs:

❑ Be certain you have sufficient cash flow during this transition period. Prepare a statement listing where money will come from and where it needs to go in the coming months. Include a list of regular bills. (See *Money Flow* on page 36.)

  ❑ Tap certain investments that may be available at face value without penalty because they carry an "estate feature" (e.g., certificates of deposit with a "death put" or a variable annuity with a death benefit greater than its current market value).

Collect benefits:

❑ Locate the birth certificate, Social Security number, marriage license, military discharge papers, financial account statements, and company benefits brochure you may need to collect certain benefits. Keep these papers readily available in your organizational folders.

❑ File a benefits claim form through the nearest Social Security office or go online at www.ssa.gov if you qualify for benefits. Call 1-800-772-1213 and ask for Publication No. 05-10084: *Social Security Survivor Benefits.* If your husband paid into the Social Security system for at least 40 quarters (10 years) and was eligible to receive Social Security, you will receive a lump-sum death benefit of $255. Unmarried children under age 18 (or older if attending high school or if disabled) are eligible for benefits, and if you are caring for these children you may qualify for survivor benefits. You can apply for Social Security retirement benefits as early as age 60 if you are a widow with limited employment income (or in some cases, even earlier).

❑ Contact your life insurance agent to start collecting benefits. You may have various payment options. Be certain you understand your choices before selecting the payout method. Check the following sources for other life insurance: your husband's employer or former employers, insurance through your mortgage company, credit cards or certain other loans, and professional association or unions.

❑ Collect veterans' benefits if you qualify. Contact the Department of Veteran Affairs if your husband served in the military. You and children of active-duty or retired military may be eligible for certain benefits, such as medical care, commissary exchange, and veterans' mortgage life insurance. For more information on benefits and procedures, go to www.va.gov or visit a local VA office.

❑ Roll over your husband's Individual Retirement Plans (IRAs) into your own. Or, if you are younger than 59½ years old and need extra income, consider making his account a beneficiary IRA. This will minimize income tax you'll pay on early distributions. (Other exceptions may exist. Consult your professional advisors before making choices.)

❏ Contact the Human Resources Department of your late husband's employer if he was employed at the time of death. Staff can assist you with unpaid salary, vacation pay, sick pay, medical-care flex or reimbursement account, bonuses and commissions, life insurance, pension benefits, access to qualified retirement accounts, stock options, and any other benefits due. If the death was because of an accident on the job, there may be accidental death benefits.

❏ Take a pension from your husband's qualified retirement plan or roll over money into your IRA, depending on your options. Review his employer's retirement plan document.

❏ Contact the financial aid office if you have a child in college. Your son or daughter may be eligible for special assistance or increased financial aid.

Adjust health and other insurance coverage:

❏ Make sure you have your own medical insurance coverage. If you and your family were covered under your deceased husband's policy at work, inquire about continuing under the group plan through COBRA coverage. (You are eligible to enroll for up to 36 months after your husband's death — more than the standard 18-month period.) You will have to pay the premium. Another option may be to convert from existing group coverage to an individual plan. If you previously had your own policy, notify the agent of your husband's death so premiums may be reduced. Notify Medicare if covered.

❏ Inform insurance agents for your auto, homeowners, liability, long-term care, and any other policies. Premiums may be reduced for one fewer driver. If your husband had long-term care insurance, you may be eligible for a return of part of his most recent premium payment.

Review assets and liabilities:

❏ Create a financial net worth statement, a list of all you own and what you owe (See *Your Net Worth* on page 38.)

Complete the estate settlement:

❏ Change the title and beneficiaries, at the appropriate time, on investments, vehicles, and your safe deposit box. It may not be necessary to change the title on your residence, depending on how it's titled now. You may want to hold off temporarily on changing names on credit cards so you can continue to use the existing cards. (When you are ready to change ownership of a credit card, write a letter to this effect and send this to the company, along with a death certificate.)

❑ Don't change your joint checking account name for a year or so because checks may still come payable to your spouse for some time. You'll be able to deposit these into your joint account.

❑ File an estate tax return with the help of your attorney if federal or state estate tax is owed (due nine months after death).

Take care of yourself:

❑ Remember self-care, which may include exercise, yoga, meditation, facials, manicures, massages, bubble baths, enjoying a beautiful sunset, spiritual practices, and chocolate! Do not let this slide!

❑ Read a good book about widowhood in general, which may give you guidance and inspiration. Here's one to start with: *For Widows Only!* by Annie Estlund (iUniverse, Inc., 2003).

❑ Consider joining a support group for widows or talking with a counselor. Several website support groups for widows are also available. One excellent location is www.widowsbond.com.

❑ Keep in touch with your women friends.

In the future, move forward with new goals and your new life:

❑ Create an updated financial plan. Focus on short-term goals first, especially during the first year or so. Keep your plan simple and manageable.

❑ Update your will and estate plan. You may want to include charitable bequests for those organizations that you and your husband supported previously.

❑ Think about writing a legacy letter (also known as an ethical will) that passes on your values, beliefs, hopes for the next generation, insights, special stories, history, and so much more.

❑ Expand your social circles. Meet new people who know you as yourself and not as half of the couple you were before your husband died.

❑ Be careful about "coupling" too quickly, if you are interested in a new relationship. Give yourself some time. Be wary of guys looking for a "purse." Keep your finances to yourself.

❑ Try to keep in mind that there is life after grief. You will be able to reframe parts of your life positively as you continue your journey as a widow.

Postpone major decisions during the first year when possible!

You don't need to rush. Especially take time with your big decisions. You are going through a grieving process, and your life may feel like it's been turned upside down. Your mental, emotional, and physical condition may be very different than before your husband's death.

Well-meaning acquaintances, extended family, or salespeople who don't really know your entire situation may bombard you with suggestions. It can be useful to have a friend help you think through some decisions you'll face. For example, now may not be the time to pay off your home mortgage. It might not be wise to move in with your adult daughter and her family either.

DON'T RUSH

If you don't want to make some decisions alone, consider asking a trusted professional to assist you. Be careful about whom you select because people who sell financial products sometimes view widows as "easy targets."

You are at a very vulnerable time following your husband's death. Go slowly. Be gentle. Give yourself time to heal.

Ask yourself this question:

Must this decision be made right now, or can it wait for a future date, which might be a better time for me to make the right choice or take action then? Just don't rush!

> **Disclaimer:** These suggested steps are generic and certainly not all inclusive for each widow's situation. Consult the advice of your attorney, accountant, and financial planner.

◆ As you read these checklists, which area do you want to work on soon?

_____

_____

_____

◆ What action will you take first? _____

_____

_____

_____

YOSEMITE SPLENDOR
STANLEY L. MOORE

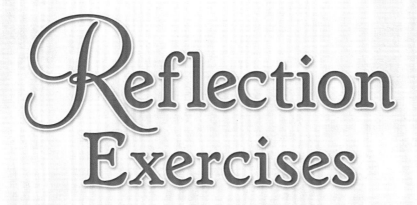

Reflection Exercises

"We can tell our values by looking
at our checkbook stubs."

~Gloria Steinem

Financial Feelings Survey

Read each statement and rate how you feel now.
Then comment about why you feel this way.

1 = I feel confident about this area
2 = I feel neutral about this area
3 = I feel uncertain or fearful about this area

Here's how I feel about:	Rating
1. My ability to manage my financial situation as a widow. COMMENTS:	
2. My ability to think clearly about money matters. COMMENTS:	
3. What I spend money on. COMMENTS:	
4. Knowing what to do with money from my husband's life insurance and other sources after his death. COMMENTS:	
5. My emotional responses to money issues. COMMENTS:	
6. My understanding of financial matters. COMMENTS:	
7. Income from my job and/or retirement income sources. COMMENTS:	
8. My financial investments. COMMENTS:	
9. Knowing I have enough money for my retirement years now or in the future. COMMENTS:	
10. Work I'm currently doing, either for pay or as a volunteer. COMMENTS:	
11. My financial recordkeeping and organization. COMMENTS:	
12. My ability to give financial help to family members if they need assistance. COMMENTS:	
13. My estate plan. COMMENTS:	

Here's how I feel about:	Rating
14. Talking about financial matters with a family member. COMMENTS:	
15. My insurance protection. COMMENTS:	
16. My debts. COMMENTS:	
17. My charitable giving. COMMENTS:	
18. My financial goals. COMMENTS:	
19. How much stress money matters cause me. COMMENTS:	
20. Professional relationships with my insurance agent, banker, financial planner, broker, tax preparer or other financial professional. COMMENTS:	

What do your responses indicate?

◆ Which area(s) do you feel most confident about? _____

_____

◆ What's an area(s) you want to improve in? _____

_____

◆ Write one thing you could do to help you feel more secure about your money life.

_____

_____

_____

For example, if you feel uncertain about your estate plan, it may be time to update your will.

◆ Circle any areas you rate as a "3," and talk about these with someone you trust. If you are in a widow's support group, ask other women how they are dealing with their misgivings about finances.

Rating Your Life Values

This exercise will help you think about what you value most in your life. Here are 16 key values that people often say they want to experience. Some say they want more of these values than others. You cannot realize them all because one may contradict another.

Assume you have to give up 11 of these values. Which would they be? Remove them by putting an "X" in the left column. Finally, rank your top five remaining value preferences, from highest (1) to lowest (5).

	Achievement	Accomplish something important in life; be involved in significant activities; succeed at what I am doing.
	Adventure	Experience variety and excitement; respond to challenging opportunities.
	Aesthetics	Appreciate and enjoy beauty for beauty's sake; be artistically creative.
	Authority/Power	Be a key decision maker, directing priorities, activities of others, and/or use of resources.
	Autonomy	Be independent, have freedom, live where I want to be and do what I want to do.
	Generosity	Give time and/or money to benefit others; express gratitude for blessings in life.
	Health	Be physically, mentally, and emotionally well; feel energetic and have a sense of well-being.
	Integrity	Be honest and straightforward, just and fair.
	Intimacy/Friendship/Love	Have close personal relationships, experience affection, share life with family and friends.
	Pleasure	Experience enjoyment and personal satisfaction from my activities.
	Recognition	Be seen as successful; receive acknowledgment for achievements.
	Security	Feel stable and comfortable with few changes or anxieties in my life.
	Service	Contribute to the quality of other people's lives and help to improve society or the world.
	Spiritual Growth	Have communication or harmony with the infinite source of life.
	Wealth	Acquire an abundance of money or material possessions; be financially rich.
	Wisdom	Have insight, pursue new knowledge, have clear judgment, and use common sense in life situations.

Put your money where your values are. Money can be a means to an end, not just the end itself. When you use your money in ways that reflect your true values, you'll probably feel happier, too.

◆ Describe a time when you felt good about spending money in a way that matched your values. _____

_____

_____

_____

_____

_____

"Price is what you pay. Value is what you get."

~*Warren Buffet*

◆ Have you ever spent money in a way that didn't support your values? If so, describe that incident. _____

_____

_____

_____

◆ Look at your number-one top value. What's one way you can use some of your money to align with this important value? _____

_____

_____

_____

_____

Note: Thanks to Ken Rouse for his kind permission to adapt this exercise from life values information in his book, Putting Money In Its Place *(Hunt Publishing Co., 1994).*

Money Flow

A money flow statement shows where your money comes from and how you spend it — for necessary and discretionary expenses. Fill in the grid below and finally complete the annual summary section to see a snapshot of your money inflows and outflows.

Income	Average Month ($)	Annual ($)
Job 1 (before withholdings)		
Job 2 (before withholdings)		
Interest		
Dividends and capital gain distributions		
Social Security		
Pension		
Income from business or partnership		
Sale of an investment or other asset		
Rental income		
Other:		
Total Income	$	$
Necessary Expenses		
Mortgage or rent		
Home maintenance		
Groceries		
Utilities and phone/Internet		
Transportation costs, gasoline, and upkeep		
Clothing and cleaning		
Personal and self-care		
Medical, dental, and other health care		
Debt or loan repayment		
Insurance: home and property		
Insurance: car		
Insurance: life		
Insurance: disability		
Insurance: long-term care		
Professional expense		
Tax: real estate		
Tax: federal		
Tax: state		
Tax withheld at work (FICA and Medicare)		
Other:		
Other:		
Total Necessary Expenses	$	$

Discretionary Expenses	Average Month ($)	Annual ($)
Vacation and leisure travel		
Dining out		
Recreation		
Entertainment		
Gifts: charitable		
Gifts: family and friends		
Home furnishings		
Savings: emergency fund		
Savings: retirement		
Savings: college		
Investments		
Family support		
Children or grandchildren		
Hobbies		
Subscriptions and dues		
Pet care		
Memberships		
Other:		
Other:		
Total Discretionary Expenses	$	$

Annual Summary	
Total Income	$
Subtract **Total Necessary Expenses**	– $
Subtract **Total Discretionary Expenses**	– $
Circle one **Excess** or **Shortage**	$

What do your numbers mean?

◆ Do you have an excess or shortage? _____

◆ If there's a shortage, can you increase income or reduce expenses? _____
  Say more about this: _____
  _____
  _____

◆ If there's an excess, what does this tell you? _____
  _____
  _____

Your Net Worth

I dentify what you own and what you owe—to determine what you're worth financially. This is referred to as your net worth statement. These numbers don't imply success or failure. It's just a snapshot of your current financial picture. Knowing this information can be a foundation to help you reach your financial goals.

ASSETS: What You Own	
Cash and Cash Equivalents	Value ($)
Checking accounts	
Savings accounts	
Money market funds	
Certificates of deposit	
Expected life insurance proceeds	
Cash value of your life insurance	
Other:	
Other:	
Retirement Assets	Value ($)
IRAs	
401(k) accounts	
Tax-deferred annuity 403(b) accounts	
457 accounts	
After-tax annuities	
Vested pension lump-sum value	
Non-qualified deferred compensation	
Other:	
Other:	
Invested Assets	Value ($)
Individual stocks	
Government bonds	
Corporate bonds	
Municipal bonds	
Mutual funds (stocks or bonds)	
Rental real estate property	
Real estate funds	
Notes receivable	
Personal loans	
Family business or nonmarketable stocks	
Other:	

Personal Use Assets	Value ($)
Primary residence	
Vacation home/Second home	
Rental property	
Other investment real estate	
Furnishings	
Automobiles	
Art, jewelry, and antiques	
Business assets	
RVs, boats, etc.	
Other:	
Total ASSETS	$

LIABILITIES: What You Owe	Value ($)
Credit cards	
Auto loans	
Primary residence mortgage	
Home equity loan/Line of credit	
Mortgage on second home	
Education loans	
Insurance loans	
Business loans	
Notes payable	
Other:	
Total LIABILITIES	$

Net Worth Calculation: Deduct liabilities from assets to determine net worth

Total ASSETS	$
Subtract **Total LIABILITIES**	– $
Equals NET WORTH	$

◆ Are you worth more, less, or about the same as you thought before completing this exercise? _____

◆ What have you done well in building your net worth? _____

_____

◆ Do you see any red flags here? _____

Family Tree

Sketch a simple family tree diagram. Start with you and your deceased husband. Then include your parents, children, and grandchildren. Add other important members of your family, such as siblings, in-laws, and others.

Your parents: _____

Your name: _____

   birth date: _____

Husband's name: _____

   birth date: _____

   date of death: _____

Date of your marriage: _____

Your child(ren): _____

_____

_____

And their spouse(s) if married: _____

_____

_____

Your grandchild(ren): _____

_____

_____

_____

Other significant family members: _____

_____

_____

◆ What are your family relationships like? _____

_____

_____

_____

_____

_____

_____

_____

_____

◆ Following your husband's death, have there been changes in family dynamics?

_____

If so, please tell what's different: _____

_____

_____

_____

_____

_____

_____

_____

_____

◆ Do your money issues also touch other members of your family? _____

_____

_____

_____

_____

_____

_____

_____

_____

SISTERS
PATRICK J. GAUGHAN

Your Money History and Style

"We can't control our destiny,
but we can control who we become."

~Anne Frank

"Real life isn't always going to be perfect or go
our way, but the recurring acknowledgement of
what is working in our lives can help us not only
to survive but surmount our difficulties."

~Sara Ban Breathnach

Money History

Growing up, we learned money messages from our parents and our communities that shaped our beliefs about money. Think about how your parents dealt with money. Were money issues openly discussed in your family or was this a subject not really talked about?

For some women, confusing or problematic issues with money, such as over-spending, hoarding, family discord, entitlement, "thinking poor," getting in debt, inability to receive, save, or follow through on good financial plans, and similar issues, may be related to their beliefs and feelings from their past.

By intentionally looking at your past and choosing which money habits you want to keep and which ones you want to leave behind, you can start to change the way you think about money going forward.

◆ What's your first memory of money? _____

_____

_____

◆ What money messages did you learn growing up? How did your parents and family deal with money? _____

_____

_____

_____

◆ What was your happiest time with money and why? _____

_____

_____

◆ What was the saddest time with money and why? _____

_____

_____

◆ Do you recognize any of your behaviors today that are related to your money history? _____ If so, are these positive or negative influences?

_____

_____

_____

What's Your Money Style?

Your beliefs about money may be based on your money history plus your more recent experience as a widow. Oftentimes we cling to beliefs about money without even thinking about why we hold them. Sometimes our money style can help us, but other times it can block progress.

Experts in this area have defined different several money styles or money personality types. Here are some examples identified by Bert Whitehead, Brent Kessell, Olivia Mellan, and others:

Guardians are always alert and careful with money issues.

Spenders prioritize pleasure and enjoyment through spending money on "the good life."

Idealists put the most value on creativity, compassion, social justice, or spiritual growth.

Hoarders seek security and abundance by accumulating more financial assets.

Stars spend, invest, or give money away to be recognized or feel classy and increase self-esteem.

Avoiders don't pay much attention to money, believing or hoping that life will work out for the best; they may feel incompetent or overwhelmed with money tasks.

Caretakers give and lend money to express compassion and generosity.

Empire builders and **entrepreneurs** thrive on power and innovation to create something of enduring value, which may include their own business.

Amassers like to have lots of money available to spend, save, or invest; they equate money with self-worth and power.

Nesters think that money invested in their homes brings happiness.

Bag ladies believe they don't have enough money and may be out on the street soon. They feel powerless to do much about their financial situation. Many widows may feel this way, at some point, even if only for a short period.

Sometimes your dominant money style can cause problems. For example, *Guardians* may prefer ultraconservative assets such as certificates of deposit and money market funds. This tendency may block their ability to build a diversified investment portfolio. For *Avoiders* whose husbands handled most of the family financial issues, it may feel strange to be in a new decision-making role at first. Recent widows may be fearful they don't have enough money and can experience the *Bag Lady* syndrome.

Ultimately, it's not about the money. Rather, it's about understanding your money and how you react so you recognize your natural inclinations toward spending, saving, giving, and investing, and what's motivating those habits. As you understand yourself better, you can make important changes to create the financial life that's best for you. Have an honest discussion with yourself about your money style. Are you a saver or a spender? Are you a penny pincher who clips coupons? Do you give too much money to your children? Are you carrying lots of credit card debt?

◆ What's your money style today? *(This may include more than one style)* _____

_____

_____

_____

◆ Has your money style changed since your husband's passing? _____
   If so, why do you think it's different now? _____

_____

_____

_____

_____

◆ Describe a positive feature of your money style: _____

_____

_____

_____

◆ What, if anything, about your money style may be problematic? _____

_____

_____

_____

_____

THE BUTTERFLY

PATRICK J. GAUGHAN

Money
Stories & More

"People say, 'What is the sense of our small efforts?' They cannot see that we must lay one brick at a time, take one step at a time."

~Dorothy Day

Enjoy a Rich Life and Not Just a Life of Riches

In *What Matters Most: Living a More Considered Life,* James Hollis says we are the most affluent culture in history, but people's souls are "starving" for the simple pleasures of life.

Hollis emphasizes that happiness and fulfillment in life do not parallel how much money we have. Rather, it's what we do beyond counting assets in our investment portfolio. It's the simple pleasures of life that really matter.

Here's a brief list of simple pleasures identified by several widows when asked what makes their lives stimulating, joyful, and fulfilling:

🍂 Get together with my girlfriends and laugh a lot

🍂 Walk my dog through a nearby pretty park

🍂 Talk with my kids by cell phone every weekend

🍂 Enjoy a café latte at Starbucks on Saturday morning with a friend

"Your success and happiness lie in you....
Resolve to keep happy, and your joy and you
shall form an invincible host against difficulties."
~Helen Keller

- Complete small daily tasks — a clean house, freshly ironed clothing, well-prepared meal
- Bake cookies with my grandchild and then eat some together
- Take my elderly neighbor to the grocery store
- Enjoy the fragrance of one gardenia as its scent fills the room
- Play a game with my young child
- Be involved with a committee that seeks to solve community problems
- Fix things for others
- See gratitude on a child's face where I do volunteer work
- Plant vegetable seeds, take care of the plants, and then enjoy eating fresh produce from my garden
- Welcome a new grandbaby into the family
- Read a great book
- Attend my high school reunion
- Watch a beautiful sunset from my backyard swing

◆ How are you leading a truly rich life? What matters most to you?

Focus on Investment Factors You Can Control

The media hypes news about people suffering as the economy sputters. The reduced value of real estate, unemployment, a credit crisis, and more distressing events have put stocks on the defensive. Avoid focusing on these and other circumstances you can't control. Rather, concentrate on what you *can* control.

Your investment performance depends on several factors:

1. How much you spend
2. How much you save
3. Length of time you're invested
4. Investing in a variety of different types of investments
5. Tax-reduction strategies
6. Informed decisions made about your new life as a widow
7. Market return

You can manage the first six variables, but number 7 is virtually impossible to control. Of course you need to pay attention to the market, but there are more pressing things to focus on, like the positives in your life.

It's like the old adage about your glass being half full or half empty. By concentrating on your values and what's really meaningful in your life, you emphasize a glass half full. It's the joy in your life that's important now and where you want to focus your energies. Pay attention to what you truly can manage, and turn away from what you have absolutely no power to control.

◆ Choose a factor from the list where you can take more control in your financial life:

_____

◆ Describe one positive step you can take in this area: _____

_____

_____

_____

_____

You Are Wealthier Than You Think

The steep cost of gasoline, high grocery bills, depressed stock prices, concerns about inflation, rising unemployment, low real estate values, rock-bottom interest rates, soaring credit card rates, and uncertain economic reports weigh heavily on many widows.

But wait. Let's put our monetary concerns in perspective. Here are some noteworthy facts you've perhaps seen before.

Did you enjoy a good meal in the past 24 hours? Do you have a place to sleep tonight? Are you wearing clothes? Answer yes, and you are wealthier than 75% of all humanity.

Got money in the bank? A few coins in your pockets? You're in the top 8% of our earth's wealthy folks. Own a house? Invest in mutual funds, stocks, bonds, and CDs? Now you've moved into the elite top range of the World's Wealthiest list.

There's more. If you attend a church, synagogue, or other place of worship without fear of harassment, arrest, torture, or death, you are more blessed than about three billion other people. Did you wake up healthy today? You're better off than the million who will not survive this week.

> "The main thing in one's own private world is to try to laugh as much as you cry."
>
> ~*Maya Angelou*

When we step back and acknowledge the abundance in our lives, we'll recognize we are wealthy indeed. We each experience riches in areas that bring us real joy — family friends, health, home, spiritual community, life purpose, and more. Yes, we are certainly very well off when we measure what's really important, along with our financial assets.

◆ Keeping everything in perspective, what special wealth do you enjoy?

_____

_____

_____

_____

"I don't want to get to the end of my life and find
that I lived just the length of it. I want to have
lived the width of it as well."

~*Diane Ackerman*

Give More Than Money to Those You Love

It has been three years since my dear mother's passing. When Mom died, she left some humble bequests, but what she experienced and learned during her 84 years was a lot more valuable. I'm blessed that Mom wrote a legacy letter. Indeed, in talking with my brother recently, he commented that he still finds it comforting to read what she wrote. I agreed.

Her two-page letter to family began, "Please know how important you are to me and how much I love you. Life has been such a fascinating and interesting adventure, with you, my family, being a big part of this journey." She continued by writing about her values, the lessons life taught her, her beliefs, and her deep love for each family member. This was Mom's story.

The money Mother left to me and my brothers will be gone soon. But her spirit, expressed on paper, will be with us forever. I treasure her timeless gift for this and future generations.

I've also written a personal legacy letter for my family. I want to give them more than my bank accounts and personal possessions. The writing process has been very nurturing and an opportunity to affirm what I care about and to renew my appreciation of life.

◆ What values, hopes, dreams, and aspirations do you want to pass on to your family?

FAMILY LEGACY

"Yesterday is history.
Tomorrow is a mystery.
Today is a gift.
That's why it's called the present."

~Eleanor Roosevelt

A "Big Grin" Goal

What would really make you happy in the coming months? What would bring you pleasure and put a huge smile on your face?

May I suggest you set what I call a "big grin" goal? It's not a New Year's resolution. Most people break those. Rather, it's a realistic goal that you can achieve.

Most "big grin" goals involve money to some extent, but the cash is secondary to the goal itself. For example, maybe you want to facilitate a family reunion and, in doing so, help your children or grandchildren with travel expenses to come join the family fun.

Or perhaps your goal is achieving better health. So you might buy a gym membership and sign up for a few sessions with a personal fitness coach as part of your plan.

Maybe it's time to redo your kitchen by brightening the color scheme and upgrading the countertops or appliances.

Traveling can be an exciting goal. It might be a series of day trips or an extended getaway. How about a week somewhere to enjoy some history, art, great food, and more? Just name a place you would like to visit and dream a little as you make your plans.

Working toward a "big grin" goal is loads of fun in itself, and, when you succeed, the sense of accomplishment, the feeling of an aspiration attained, will boost your spirits enormously. Why? Because you were the one to make it happen.

◆ What is a "big grin" goal for you? _____

_____

_____

_____

_____

_____

_____

_____

_____

_____

_____

"The very least you can do in your life is
to figure out what to hope for. And the most
you can do is live inside that hope."

~*Barbara Kingsolver*

A Free Concert in the Park

That was my Friday evening outing theme when another widow and I took a picnic basket supper to attend a fabulous free outdoor concert. (She and I both agreed to find several inexpensive ways to have fun together in our community.)

Spirited symphonic fare included Dvorak, Mozart, Berlioz, Lecuona, Bizet, Sousa, and more. There were also selections from *My Fair Lady*, a salute to Dixieland jazz, and music from *Star Wars*. The performance ended with Tchaikovsky's ever-popular *1812 Overture*.

Several hundred people gathered under spreading oak trees with their lawn chairs, with festive food and beverages galore. We even ran into other friends we knew there. It was one glorious event, and it was absolutely free!

Make a game of finding inexpensive or free activities. Consider art gallery hops, community festivals, educational seminars, and Fourth of July fireworks. Or you may prefer walking tours at historic sites, poetry readings in a local bookstore, strolling along the beach, and get-togethers with friends for a decadent dessert and conversation at a special restaurant.

Peruse the weekend section of your local newspaper to find inviting seasonal activities in your community, or look online to locate enjoyable and inexpensive outings nearby. In short, participate in fun events that are also easy on your wallet.

◆ Find a free or inexpensive event in your area and make plans to participate. Maybe you'll invite a girlfriend or relative to go with you. How do you feel about saving money this way? _____

_____

_____

_____

_____

_____

_____

"O how I laugh when I think of my vague
indefinite riches. No run on my bank
can drain it, for my wealth is not
possession but enjoyment."

~Henry David Thoreau

Buy Experiences and Invest in Memories

The week before Labor Day I brought family members together for a special reunion. I rented a historic log cabin along the shores of Lake Michigan. There was a boat-filled harbor with many special attractions for us to enjoy, including good food, a weekend music festival, bike trails, and art galleries.

But even better, we had time to walk and talk along the lake, cherish lingering conversations over cups of fragrant tea, share stories about my adult children's dreams for their futures, collapse into gales of laughter, view old family photo albums, go kayaking, bike together in a pretty park, enjoy treats in an old-fashioned ice cream parlor, and so much more. It was a special time to affirm and strengthen our family bonds.

I picked up the tab for the weekend expenses, including my children's transportation to the event. I did this because I knew I was getting a great return on this "investment."

You might also want to think about how to spend some of your money to "buy experiences and invest in memories." This is one way to match your values with your financial resources.

Forget for the moment the futility of purchasing stuff to please those who probably don't need more things. Instead, consider buying a special event, an interesting adventure, or a shared activity that can result in happy memories lasting a lifetime. It's truly a gift that keeps on giving forever.

◆ What's one way you could buy experiences and invest in memories?

"Give thanks for a little and you
will find a lot."

~Hausa proverb from Nigeria

Put Your Gratitude into Action!

When good things happen to us, we feel grateful. For example, we are thankful for our family, a comfortable home, caring friends, meaningful employment, good health, life in a free country, a pretty sunset, and much more. When we stop to count all our blessings, we would likely say we've received lots to be thankful for.

I believe feeling thankful is a crucial first step. But the next step is to be actively grateful rather than just passively grateful. For me, that means doing something to show my gratitude. So I give to others, just as I have received. My giving is an active response to all the good I have already received and will be given in the future.

Active gratitude might be writing a note of thanks to my neighbor who invited me for a cup of tea or spending time with an ill friend. Opening my purse is another way I can say "thank you" for the good in my life. It's simply healthy for me to give. Indeed, giving isn't so much about the receiver who benefits from my gift. It's more about me as the giver. I give because expressing gratitude makes me feel good.

Charitable giving allows me to express my gratitude in a very tangible way. I know my gifts make a difference in the lives of others. My late husband and I established the Rehl Family Scholarship Fund many years ago, following the tragic death of our daughter. Giving in this way helped our healing process. I've received heartwarming letters from our scholarship recipients. It really makes me feel good to give. Yes, I got a great emotional return on this financial philanthropic investment.

After my husband died, I added memorial gift money to our Fund. After I pass on, another gift will be made from my estate to enable even more scholarships in the future.

You may also want to express gratitude by making charitable gifts both now and in your estate plan to organizations special to you. These may include religious groups, educational institutions, children's causes, health research, cultural arts associations, care and support groups, world hunger relief, homeless shelters, senior services, humanitarian causes, animal-related organizations, or others.

Giving your volunteer time and talents is also a good way to express gratitude.

◆ What's one way you can practice active gratitude? _____

_____

_____

"I've always known that life is better when you
share it. I now realize it gets even sweeter
when you expand the circle."

~Oprah

Write Your New Will and Other Estate Planning Documents

My husband died in February 2007. Then my dear mother passed a month later. I deeply miss their physical presence, but their spirits and love will always be with me. I'm grateful for my faith in God, along with friends, family, and clients who offered loving support during that transition time.

Yes, managing grief at the death of a loved one is difficult. You may have experienced a similar intense heartache like mine when your husband died.

As the executor of my husband's and my mother's wills, I had two estates to settle. That was pretty straightforward work, although time consuming. They both did almost everything right in terms of their end-of-life planning.

Writing a will that clearly explains your final wishes is a lasting gift for those you leave behind. What a meaningful bequest for your loved ones! It could be called "tying up the loose ends of our lives." In addition to a will, you may also have a trust. Have you completed a living will and appointed a health-care advocate to make decisions about your treatment if you have a terminal illness? Have you given durable power of attorney to someone you trust who would help with financial decisions if necessary? If you have young children, have you made provisions for their care if you die prematurely? Left undone, incomplete estate plans may cause pain, guilt, sorrow, and regret for family members. That's on top of the grief they feel. Ouch!

It's been said that half of all lawyers die with unfinished estate plans. That's understandable. Preparing for one's death demands that you confront a toxic mix of chaotic emotions and enervating details.

As you think about your own end-of-life plans, are all of your loose ends tied up? Doing so is a great final gift for those you care for. And that includes telling people you love them — today. Waiting until sometime in the future may be too late.

◆ Have you updated your will, following your husband's death? _____

◆ If your estate plans are incomplete, what is one step you could take soon to make progress in this area? _____

_____

_____

_____

Rusty Red Water

I saw it immediately as I drove into my garage after returning from an enjoyable evening out with friends. There it was — rusty red water, slowly seeping across the sloping concrete floor.

My eyes followed the meandering mess back to its source. My hot water heater was hemorrhaging this nasty fluid from a top valve. The stuff slithered down the side of the tank, leaving a rusty streak before hitting the floor and spreading out. Yuck!

"I am not afraid of storms, for I am learning how to sail my ship."

~Louisa May Alcott

My first thought was, "Am I jinxed or what?" That's because just a few days before, at 2 AM, my home security system had malfunctioned, setting off an ear-splitting alarm and simultaneously sending a "panic" code to the sheriff. Within minutes a law enforcement officer was at my front door, with me in my robe explaining I was OK. Just a false alarm, which still required a service call the following day. And the week before, one of my computers went on the blink. That also resulted in a repair technician's visit.

So as I watched that red rusty water flowing, I knew I would be contacting yet another fix-it guy. Before going to bed I looked for a plumber on Craigslist and checked the yellow pages. Too many choices and too late at night, so I finally just went to sleep.

Next morning I woke up hoping that maybe I had imagined the problem or the water heater had miraculously healed itself overnight. No such luck. Peeking into the garage, I saw that the rusty water was oozing even faster from the water heater. Better make a decision soon, I thought, because the tank might blow like a geyser.

But just as I was about to select a plumber at random from the yellow pages, I heard a guardian angel whisper, "Check the warranty. There's a file in the green cabinet." So I did just that and found the water heater manual, including a phone number to call.

I contacted the manufacturer and to my delight learned that my warranty had four months to go before expiration. The helpful service rep put me in touch with a local plumber, who came to my house that same afternoon. He efficiently replaced my water heater with a brand-new unit for free, with only a small service call fee. Within a short time clean hot water was running through my home faucets again.

Life is like this. Stuff breaks. And it's not just the stuff of life that is challenging. It might be a broken relationship, a job lost, a dream unfulfilled, a debilitating physical problem, death of your spouse or another loved one, or _____ (you fill in the blank). Life is full of imperfections. Sometimes we can fix these things with the help of a good repair person, or friends who care, or family members who are there to love and support us. Sometimes a guardian angel intervenes. But then there are times when we can't fix the situation, and we learn to adapt and go on because that's part of life, too.

I've been blessed with good "repair folks" since my husband's death, and I'm grateful for them. I hope you also have these resources to lean on when you need them. I'll bet there are even times when you've been a repair person for somebody else and have helped them, too.

◆ Start a list of good repair folks, including their phone numbers. If you are in a support group, you may want to exchange names of reputable plumbers, electricians, painters, lawn care specialists, house cleaners, handymen or women, etc. that others recommend. _____

_____

_____

_____

_____

_____

_____

_____

_____

_____

_____

_____

"One of life's most fulfilling moments occurs in
the split-second when the familiar is suddenly
transformed into the dazzling aura of
the profoundly new."

~*Edward B. Lindaman*

Pennies from Heaven

Many folks have asked me, *"Are you still finding those pennies, Kathleen?"* I want to share my penny story with you. First you need to know that I occasionally found coins when I walked years ago with my husband, Tom. No big deal; everybody finds coins periodically.

Now it is a rare occasion if I do not find a penny, quarter, nickel, dime, or even a Susan B. Anthony dollar when I go walking. I'm serious! It's seldom I return home with empty pockets. My best find during an hour-long walk was eight coins in seven different spots along the way.

There's more to this penny tale. I won't go into all the details, but it has to do with a connection I felt with Tom a few days after his passing. Indeed, on that first solo walk without my partner, I found a $100 bill blowing down an empty side street! I sensed Tom's playful self nearby. When I saw the words "In God We Trust" on the back of that bill, I knew where the breeze came from that blew that gift to me. It's a keeper. I'll never spend it.

Each time I continue to find pennies, a smile floods my face … and I think of my good-humored Tom. It's comforting to fantasize that maybe, just maybe, this is his way of staying in touch with me from heaven. (I smile, thinking that he knows how connected I am with money in my work as a financial advisor.)

◆ Have you felt a gentle connection with your husband after his death, through a memory or event? _____

_____

_____

_____

_____

_____

_____

Wheel of Life

Place a dot in each section of the wheel, indicating your satisfaction with this part of your life.

I f you feel very positive about this aspect of the wheel, put your dot near the segment's outer green boundary line, closer to the 10. If you don't feel so good about this area of your life, place your dot near the circle's center, which represents a zero. Are your feelings somewhere in between? Then put your dot at an intermediate spot. Finally, connect all your dots together going around the circle.

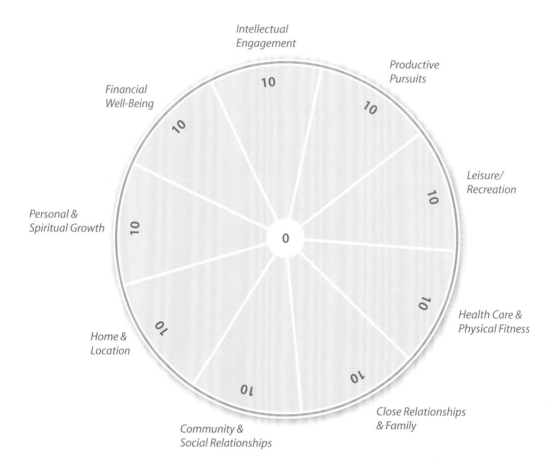

When you connect the dots, is the resulting shape a balanced circle, or do you have jagged parts of your life that are out of balance?

For example, if your "Health Care & and Physical Fitness" dot is nearer the center of this circle, it may reflect a lack of exercise or eating habits that aren't good. Select one segment of this wheel of life where you would like to improve.

◆ What segment do you want to focus on? _____

_____

◆ Now identify one small step you can make soon, which will help move your dot closer to the green edge of the circle, closer to a rating of 10. For example, if you selected the "Personal & Spiritual Growth" segment, maybe reading an uplifting article would encourage you. _____

_____

_____

_____

_____

_____

_____

◆ What is the positive action step you'll take soon? Also note if this may or may not involve a financial cost. _____

_____

_____

_____

_____

_____

_____

_____

◆ What is today's date? _____

◆ After completing your one activity successfully,
note this date also: _____

"When it is dark enough,
you can see the stars."

~*Ralph Waldo Emerson*

Other Things to Think About

I deliberately limited the scope of this guidebook. My focus was to encourage you to start moving on some important matters related to your money and financial issues without overwhelming you. I've listed some other specialized financial topics you may want to learn more about when you are ready to take additional steps forward.

With comprehensive financial planning you'll look at multiple financial concerns together at the same time. The result is a strategy for accomplishing your goals that is implemented and monitored over time. Your special issues may include:

* *Decluttering your life.* Learn to improve your financial recordkeeping, including what to keep, what to pitch, and what to update. This can include debt reduction.

* *Insurance planning.* Review your life insurance, health insurance, home, vehicle, disability, long-term care coverage, and other types of insurance. Carefully consider your options before buying additional life insurance, to determine your true need for this coverage. For example, if your children are grown and you have no dependents, you may want to adjust your level of coverage.

* *Income tax planning.* In the year your husband died, you can file a joint income tax return. For two years after the year of your husband's death, you may be eligible to file as a qualifying widow with dependent child. Otherwise you will file as single or head of household. By carefully planning your deductions and credits, you may be able to save money on your tax return.

* *Investment planning.* You'll develop a plan that matches your age and stage in life, with an appropriate functional allocation of investments including stocks, bonds, money market funds, certificates of deposit, and more. Be careful that you choose assets that are really right for your situation, rather than buying investments you do not understand.

* *Retirement planning.* If you are still employed, you'll want to look toward the time when you no longer work for a living and what you'll need to do to prepare for that financial transition.

* *Children and money matters.* If you have adult children, they may ask you to relocate closer to them or want you to move into their home. Don't make this decision hurriedly because there are long-term implications. If you have young children, you may want to plan for their future education costs.

◆ What's an important money issue you want to learn more about? _____

_____

_____

Finding a Financial Advisor

You may already be working with a trusted financial professional. If that's the case, you probably don't need to read this section. However, if you do not yet enjoy this helpful relationship, you may benefit from speaking with an advisor about your situation. If you would like to experience financial peace of mind, where you feel safe and secure about your money issues, a good planner can help you achieve this goal.

You'll want to identify a qualified professional who will be a real "thinking partner" to help you make decisions — someone who listens with empathy and respect, whom you trust completely.

This advisor will be able to provide comprehensive financial planning, which is more than just money management and a retirement plan. Comprehensive planning may include buying a car, taking advantage of all tax deductions, analyzing income and expenses, refinancing a home mortgage, acquiring the right types and amount of insurance, planning for a child's education, deciding when to start Social Security income, estate and legacy planning, business planning, selecting the right investments, charitable giving, making values-based money decisions, and so much more. Indeed, every aspect of your life related to money should be part of your financial plan.

Look for an advisor with an accepted professional designation. The most widely acknowledged credential is the CFP® (Certified Financial Planner) status.

Select an advisor who puts your interest first as he or she provides unbiased and holistic advice. The *Wall Street Journal, New York Times, Kiplinger's, Money magazine,*

and *AARP publications* counsel readers to work with advisors who are paid a fee for their services.

If you pay a fee, it may be a flat retainer amount, an hourly fee, or a project rate. Another method of fee payment is a percentage of the value of assets the advisor manages for you. Your planner may also receive commissions from the firm he or she represents. Advisors can explain to you how they are compensated.

Be wary of an investment product that sounds too good to be true, because it probably is. Carefully read and understand disclaimers about marketing and advertising materials.

You can locate qualified planners through the Alliance of Cambridge Advisors (www. acaplanners.org), Financial Planning Association (www.fpanet.org), Garrett Planning Network (www.garrettplanningnetwork.com), National Association of Personal Financial Advisors (www.napfa.org), and Sudden Money Institute (www.suddenmoney. com). Working with a credentialed, ethical financial advisor well versed in the special needs of widows can make your difficult transition as a widow more manageable.

After narrowing your choices, schedule a meeting with several advisors. To find the best fit, consider their credentials, background, experience, and specialties. Do they work with other widows? Also pay attention to their listening and communication skills.

You may want to bring a close family member or friend when you meet with a prospective advisor, especially if you are in the early phases of widowhood. That way you'll have two sets of ears to evaluate your meeting.

If you don't locate a financial advisor in your immediate area who works with widows, it's possible to find a long-distance financial planner who can coach you by phone. Know that help is available, wherever you live.

◆ Who might accompany you when you meet with a potential financial planner?

◆ What questions will you ask a potential financial advisor?

"Joy is prayer. Joy is strength. Joy is love.
Joy is a net of love by which you can catch souls."

~*Mother Teresa*

Index

"It's not so much that we're afraid of change or
so in love with the old ways,
but it's that place in between that we fear …
It's like being in between trapezes.
It's Linus when his blanket is in the dryer.
There's nothing to hold on to."

~*Marilyn Ferguson*

Notes

_____
_____
_____
_____
_____
_____
_____
_____
_____
_____
_____
_____
_____
_____
_____
_____
_____
_____

"A friend is someone who knows the song in your heart, and can sing
it back to you when you have forgotten the words."

~*Donna Roberts*